JOKES
FOR
MINECRAFTERS

BOOBY TRAPS, BOMBS, BOO-BOOS, AND MORE

MICHELE C. HOLLOW, JORDON P. HOLLOW, AND STEVEN M. HOLLOW

Illustrations by Amanda Brack

Bloomsbury is a registered trademark of Bloomsbury Publishing Plc

Copyright © 2016 by Skyhorse Publishing, Inc. 2016

Minecraft® is a registered trademark of Notch Development AB.
The Minecraft game is copyright © Mojang AB.

ISBN 978-1-4088-7787-6

A CIP catalogue for this book is available from the British Library.

Printed by CPI Group (UK) Ltd, Croydon CR0 4YY

MIX
Paper from
responsible sources
FSC® C020471
www.fsc.org

1 3 5 7 9 10 8 6 4 2

CONTENTS

INTRODUCTION

Minecraft is a lot like a foreign language. Those of you holding this book are fluent in Minecraft-speak while others who have never played this awesome game will need someone like you to translate these jokes for them. We hope you enjoy these Minecraft jokes, riddles, limericks, tongue twisters, haikus, trivia, and mottos that we'd like to see. Maybe you will see yourself in the "Boo-Boos Made by Noobs" and in the "You Might Be a Minecraft Addict If . . ." chapters.

As you know, there are so many layers in Minecraft. While we've dug deep, there's still a lot of ground to cover. Why not come up with your own Minecraft jokes to share with your friends? It's a lot of fun, and while you are reading this book, we hope you have many laughs. Just remember, "Sss, boom!" Never hug a creeper!

CHAPTER 1

BOOBY TRAPS AND BOMBS

JOKES

Q: Where did the creeper go after the explosion?
A: Everywhere!

■

Q: What did the player say when he blew up the creeper?
A: "Dynamite!"

■

Q: Why do creepers like Rice Krispies?
A: Because they go *snap, crackle, POP!*

■

Q: What goes "Sneak, sneak, sss! Kaboom!"?
A: A creeper with a bomb in his hands!

Q: What do you get when you cross a creeper with a bomb?

A: A bomb that sneaks up on you!

■

Q: Why don't they have knock-knock jokes in Minecraft?

A: Because hostile mobs don't knock on your door. They blow it up!

Q: How did Steve feel after he stepped on a landmine?

A: He felt *de-feeted*.

Q: What is a Minecraft player's favourite TV show?

A: *The Big Bang Theory!*

■

Q: What do you get if you cross a creeper with a monkey?

A: A ba-BOOM!

■

Q: What did the player say on his way to a creeper rock concert?

A: "I hope I don't get blown away!"

■

Q: How do you make a creeper shower?

A: Give him a hand grenade!

■

Q: What film do Minecraft players like to watch?

A: *The Terminator.*

■

Q: What do you call a cow that eats a bomb?

A: Udder destruction!

Q: What would you get if a famous French emperor stepped on a landmine?

A: Napoleon Blownapart!

Q: What did the player say after falling into a booby trap?

A: "That was a blast!"

Q: What do you call a creeper with a bomb in his hands?

A: It doesn't matter; he will be blown to smithereens!

First player: "What you don't know won't hurt you."

Second player: "Tell that to the player who just landed on a booby trap!"

■

First Player: "Did you hear about the player who covered a lot of territory?"

Second Player: "No. How'd that happen?"

First Player: "He stepped on a booby trap and is all over the place!"

■

First player: "Building landmines is an expensive hobby."

Second player: "Why?"

First player: "It can cost an arm and a leg!"

■

First player: "I never wanted to follow in Steve's footsteps."

Second player: "Why?"

First player: "Because he stepped on a landmine!"

■

First player: "So far, I've bombed ten creepers!"

Second player: "Sounds like you're having a blast tonight!"

First player: "What happens if you swallow uranium?"
Second player: "You get *atomic ache*."

■

First player: "Did you see all of the Minecraft merchandise in the shops and online?"
Second player: "Yes, it's a booming industry!"

■

First player: "Did you hear about the book that fell on the player's head?"
Second player: "How did it happen?"
First player: "He only had his-*shelf* to blame!"

■

First player: "How is Minecraft different from LEGO?"
Second player: "LEGO doesn't have bombs or booby traps!"

■

First player: "Did you hear about the player who thought the creeper was giving out free hugs?"
Second player: "No, what happened?"
First player: "He went *KABOOM*!"

Q: How fun was the Minecraft party?
A: It was a blast!

■

First player: "Did you hear about the player who built a fireplace inside his TNT house?"
Second player: "No."
First player: "Really? He was all over town."

First player: "Did you hear about the player who heated his house with lava?"

Second player: "Was he burned to a crisp?"

First player: "No, he just went with the flow."

■

First player: "I just saw a new player destroy a thousand creepers."

Second player: "Wow! That sounds amazing."

First player: "It was good, but I wasn't blown away!"

■

Knock, knock.

Who's there?

Hand grenade.

Hand grenade who?

Kaboom!

TONGUE TWISTERS

Brad borrowed Betty's bombs.

Bobby blasted big black bats.

Bombs being built by Billy.

Terry targets tyrants with TNT.

Cam creams creepy creepers crawling 'cross the carpet.

Clever Carole caught creepers—*kaboom*!

Before bombs burst, back off!

Betty borrowed Bonnie's big bomb!

MINECRAFT LIMERICKS, POEMS, AND HAIKUS

There once was a player named Jay.
He was having a very bad day.
A mob of creepers attacked.
They just wouldn't stay back.
And sad Jay was all blown away!

■

A blaze swooped in with fireballs blazing.
Some cows nearby were grazing.
The blaze was caught in a trap,
He most surely did snap,
And the explosion was quite amazing.

■

While being pursued on a beach,
The player created a breach.
He threw his last bomb
And escaped without harm,
From the creeper, he was now out of reach.

■

A player tried to retreat.
The situation looked like defeat.
A nearby big ghast
Shot fireballs that blast
And hit him on his very big feet.

■

As explosions lit up the night,
Bombs burst with all of their might.
A zombie, quite young,
Stuck out his tongue
And dared me to come over and fight.

■

I threw a bomb from way up high.
It fell from the dark night sky.
Mobs of ghasts were down below.
Hitting them, I waved hello.
One escaped with a great big sigh.

■

The bomb I made was first class.
No other could ever surpass.
Armed with such power,
I vowed I would shower
A creeper that was giving me sass.

■

A bold player on a new mission
Had untested bombs in his munitions.
Would they be sound?
Would creepers hit the ground?
Yeah, his plan came to fruition!

■

Watch where you travel.
Beware, don't step on gravel.
It's a booby trap!

■

Beware, be careful.
Booby traps are hidden here,
And there, and there, too!

■

Did you hear that sound?
Oh no, a ticking time bomb!
Last sound was *kaboom*!

■

A zombie chased me from the start.
He almost captured my beating heart.
A booby trap I laid
Was the price he had paid.
Now, he's in many body parts!

■

A legendary player named Pap
Hit targets while taking a nap.
Such precision and ease,
Mobs he could tease
And trick them with hidden booby traps!

■

A mob of zombies hid down by the creek.
For our hero, the world looked bleak.
Hostile mobs kept on forming,
Strange creatures were swarming.
Poor hero ran out of bombs last week.

■

This battle was not what I planned.
I had to attack the zombie by hand.
Behind him I crept,
And I could have wept,
Because my bomb fell into the sand!

■

There once was a player named Nero.
He wanted to feel like a hero.
He bombed a hostile mob
And made this his job.
His chances were greater than zero!

■

He built a booby trap kit
And waited for mobs to steal it.
For in it was a bomb.
Outside it seemed quite calm.
Opened, the mob would get hit.

■

The bomb the player built was a brute.
He disguised it to look rather cute.
His trap he did set
While making a bet
That the creeper would explode en route!

■

A player with a big smile
Built a bomb projectile.
If stepped on just right,
The enemy would take flight
And would explode in great style!

■

A player planned all through daylight
Of the creepers he would bomb in the night.
Large numbers gathered and grew,
Soon there would be just a few.
In blasting them he took great delight!

■

I launched a giant bomber.
This creeper would be a goner.
He fought with great might—
A terrible fight.
He lost, and now I'm much calmer!

■

There once was a player named Tom.
He got hold of a very large bomb.
It blew up in his face.
He was flung into space.
Now, that's the end of poor Tom.

RIDDLES, PUNS, AND MINECRAFT PHRASES

I take just four seconds to explode. What am I?
TNT!

I can scare creepers and I'm not TNT. What am I?
A cat!

Puns about Minecraft mishaps can be classified as *a leg gory*.

Landmines. Where do you stand on them?

As I stood on a landmine, I thought, *My feet are killing me!*

If everything in Minecraft is square, how do you get a *round* of ammo?

Hey, I wonder if this could be one of those booby . . .
Kaboom!

CHAPTER 2

BOO-BOOS MADE BY NOOBS

TONGUE TWISTERS

Noobs know Nether, not nexus.

No, not never know Nether.

Noobs Nancy, Ned, and Nathan needed Nether wart.

Patty poorly poured potions.

Sheila saw six sheep sleeping.

Steve's sword sliced squid.

Ghasts got Gary grounded.

MINECRAFT LIMERICKS, POEMS, AND HAIKUS

Think back and recall
The first time you played Minecraft.
We can see you smile!

■

There once was a noob named Chuck.
He completely ran out of luck.
He tripped over his cat
And fell into a vat.
Now he is covered in muck.

■

There once was a noob named Paul.
He fought a creeper and gave it his all.
He escaped from a cave
By digging sideways
Then triggered a massive rock fall.

■

There once was a noob named Clive
Who escaped by taking a nosedive!
He landed in a vat.
His body went splat!
Ah, poor Clive is no longer alive!

■

A noob crept out onto the field.
He hid behind a sheep as he kneeled.
A ghast took direct aim.
The dim noob was slain.
For a sheep makes a terrible shield.

A new player that wasn't so brave
Hid deep, deep in a cave.
His bright torch—a mistake—
Caused spiders to wake.
He retreated and gave them a wave.

■

Take this wise advice:
Jump in and play without fear.
You will have much fun!

■

A noob was crossing the street,
Searching for villagers to meet.
Instead, he confronted a ghast.
He tried to run past,
But was caught and suffered defeat!

■

The noob started out quite well.
Players rallied around and would yell:
"Hurray for the noob that defeats all the mobs!"
With potions, converted them to gooey globs,
Which he slipped on, tumbled, and fell!

■

There once was a noob named Bob.
He successfully slaughtered a mob.
He fell into a hole,
Was impaled on a pole.
Now Bob's a human kebab!

■

There once was a noob named Sam.
In the water he went and swam.
A zombie nearby
Caught his twinkling eye
And is eating Sam like a ham.

■

An unwise noob laid in waiting.
A creeper, he was baiting.
Soon spotted was he,
Crouching down by a tree.
Now his life is quickly fading!

∎

There once was a noob named Ned.
He didn't use his head.
Bringing water into the Nether
Wasn't very clever.
Being so thirsty, he fled.

∎

A noob passed through a portal.
It almost made him feel immortal.
He defeated a ghast
And had the last laugh
And made this noob snort and chortle.

∎

A noob as strong as an ox
Loved playing with Minecraft blocks.
He created a village,
Which a creeper did pillage.
His world was reduced to just rocks.

■

There once was a noob named Bob.
He spotted his very first mob.
He thought they looked cute.
Instead they were brutes
Who made griefing him their job.

■

Please don't blame the noob.
You were one some time ago.
We learn from mistakes.

■

Noobs always improve.
If they try and don't give up
They just get better.

■

If success is far
And just feels beyond your reach,
Just keep on trying!

■

There once was a noob named Nancy.
Playing Minecraft was her fancy.
With gusto, she burrowed straight down.
Broke her pickaxe, which caused her to frown.
Now Nancy's agitated and antsy.

■

Think noobs know nothing?
They will try and try again
And have lots of fun!

DID YOU HEAR . . . ?

Did you hear about the noob who looked an Enderman right
in the eyes?
He searched the site for sunglasses!

Did you hear about the noob who built a fire in her wooden house?
The entire house went up in flames!

Did you hear about the noob who spent days trying to get his minecart to move and finally realized he had to power the rails?
He went nowhere!

Did you hear about the player who thought he was too powerful to need armour or swords?
What a noob!

Did you hear about the noob who thought the pool of lava was gold?
He respawned to tell the tale!

Did you hear about the noob who touched a cactus?
He's all scratched up!

Did you hear about the noob who tried to hypnotize an Enderman?
He was destroyed.

Did you hear about the noob whose favourite block is air?
Nothing happened!

Did you hear about the noob who thought a bed of lava was a hot tub?
It destroyed him!

Did you hear about the noob who put on armour but forgot her sword?
It ended poorly!

Did you hear about the noob who hugged a creeper?
He went boom!

Did you hear about the noob who punched a tree?
Her fists are full of splinters!

Did you hear about the noob who tossed meat to a creeper?
No one's seen him since!

Did you hear about the noob who mistook lava for a pool of water?
He sure learned his lesson!

Did you hear about the noob who climbed a tree to escape a ghast?
Unfortunately, he didn't see the other mobs hiding in that tree!

Did you hear about the noob who spent hours mining obsidian with a wood pick?
He was board to death!

Did you hear about the noob who built a dirt house with no torches?
In seconds it was filled with skeletons!

Did you hear about the noob who learned the hard way that you can't kill a ghast with a sword?
She was destroyed!

Did you hear about the noob who made a monster trap in Peaceful mode?
She didn't know why monsters didn't spawn!

Did you hear about the noob who went out exploring and forgot where her home was?
She is still looking!

Did you hear about the noob who kept on calling the health icon a heart?
She tried to draw smiley faces on the screen, too!

Did you hear about the noob who spent hours pressing the arrow key in order to move?
He went nowhere!

Did you hear about the noob who changed the words to Taio Cruz's song "Dynamite" so that it mentions Minecraft?
Her popularity has exploded all over the Internet.

Did you hear about the noob who shot an arrow into the air?
He missed!

Did you hear about the noob who tested TNT in her house?
She rocked the roof!

Did you hear about the noob who built a hotel in the Nether?
His guests thought his beds were a real blast!

Did you hear about the noob who kept on bugging her friend to share recipes?
She now makes a tasty spider stew!

Did you hear about the noob who actually invited a creeper into his house because he didn't know what it was?
His house blew up!

Did you hear about the noob who was running so fast that he didn't see the edge of the cliff?
He respawned!

Did you hear about the player who was so freaked out that when she was attacked by a few mobs she forgot to use her sword?
What a noob.

Did you hear about the noob who worked so hard to gather gold, only to drop it when he was chased into a ravine to escape hostile mobs?
He is still searching for it.

Did you hear about the noob who tried to mine stones with a hoe?
All the other players laughed, "Ho, ho, ho."

Did you hear about the noob who spent fifteen hours trying to craft a saddle?
I don't know wither or not she ever finished!

Did you hear about the noob who forgot to turn on the sound?
He couldn't hear the creeper. . . .

Did you hear about the noob who thought the Enderman looked friendly?
He was destroyed!

Did you hear about the noob who spent the entire day gathering wood and didn't craft it into wooden planks?
He got board!

Did you hear about the noob who tried to sleep in a bed in the Nether?
She had one of those dreams where you're falling right after you get blown up!

Did you hear about the noob who tried to mine a diamond with a gold pickaxe?
He's still at it!

Did you hear about the noob who forgot and turned off Peaceful mode after he placed torches all through the tunnel?
The creepers saw the light!

Did you hear about the noob who tried to dig up and hit gravel?
It was a rocky situation.

Did you hear about the noob who spent hours trying to make a torch out of a flint?
He's steel trying!

Did you hear about the noob who stood on the TNT when it went off?
It was a moving experience!

Did you hear about the noob who burned leaves too close to his house?
He was left with nothing.

Did you hear about the player who left the door open and then creepers came to visit!
What a noob.

Did you hear about the noob who was so excited to build his wooden house next to the lava?
He was all fired up.

Did you hear about the noob who tried to build a bridge with sand?
He sunk!

Did you hear about the noob who built a house with only one exit?
No, but the hostile mobs did!

Did you hear about the noob who caught on fire and tried to put the flames out with a bucket of water?
Unfortunately, it was a bucket of lava!

Did you hear about the noob who mistook a zombie for a player?
He was lunch!

Did you hear about the noob who wanted to build a popular club and thought TNT was a decorative block?
It really exploded!

Did you hear about the noob who didn't know how to land in Survival mode?
He's still soaring!

Did you hear about the noob who crafted bows backward?
He became the target!

Did you hear about the noob who didn't know how to move water around?
He placed buckets all around and waited for it to rain!

Did you hear about the noob who threw a damage potion at a zombie?
Nothing happened!

Did you hear about the noob who tried to break gold blocks with his right hand?
Now they call him Lefty.

Did you meet the noob who was too afraid to venture outside even though her home was in Peaceful mode?
Of course not!

Did you hear about the noob who spent the first few minutes of nightfall running around without any weapons?
It wasn't long before she was destroyed.

Did you hear about the noob who didn't store her valuables and weapons in a chest at her base?
She was dis-armed!

Did you hear about the player who ventured into the Nether without armour or weapons?
What a noob!

Did you hear about the noob who ran into her house to hide from a creeper?
Creepers are very good at hide-and-get-blown-up!

Did you hear about the noob who thought creepers were passive mobs?
Wrong, oh so wrong!

Did you hear about the noob who built a house in a cave and forgot to build a fourth wall?
She had unexpected company!

Did you hear about the noob who didn't know he was on multiplayer and mistook a friend for a creeper?
That will teach his friend to just drop in!

Did you hear about the noob who traded diamonds for gold?
Ooh, shiny!

Did you hear about the noob who didn't pack food during the cave exploration?
It didn't end well for him!

Did you hear about the noob who built her house high up on gravel?
Everything went downhill!

Did you hear about the noob who repeatedly fell into the same lava pool five times?
She respawned over and over and over and over and over again!

Did you hear about the player who trapped himself?
What a noob!

Did you hear about the noob who built a house with an iron door that locked from the outside?
He's still inside!

Did you hear about the noob who left TNT near redstone?
Kaboom!

Did you hear about the noob who thought zombies and skeletons could survive daylight?
He hid inside his house all day!

Did you hear about the noob who decided to make a lava moat around his wooden castle?
It was flaming!

Did you hear about the noob who fought creepers with a wooden shovel?
She thought that was her strongest weapon!

Did you hear about the player who built his house in Creative mode and spotted creepers?
He hid! What a noob.

Did you hear about the noob who saw a shovel and started thinking about digging a mine in her own backyard?
Her family has a lovely new swimming pool!

Did you hear about the player who tried making tools out of redstone, lapis, and sandstone?
What a noob!

Did you hear about the noob who decided to decorate her bedroom with creeper traps?
She caught her little brother on Monday and her mum on Tuesday and was grounded for the weekend!

Did you hear about the noob who wore obsidian?
She's incredibly hot!

Did you hear about the noob who put his mum's diamond
ring on the end of a stick and tried to dig with it?
He was grounded for a week.

Did you hear about the noob who visited a farm?
*She ran away from the pigs because she thought they might
attack her!*

YOU MIGHT BE A NOOB . . .

You might be a noob if you think those hissing voices are
coming from an Ender Dragon.

You might be a noob if you spot a creeper and go outside your
house.

You might be a noob if you build a dirt house.

You might be a noob if you pet a wolf.

You might be a noob if you mistake redstone for rubies.

CHAPTER 3

LAVA, DROWNING, AND OTHER DASTARDLY WAYS TO DIE

JOKES

Q: How are cacti like creepers?

A: You can't hug either of them!

■

Q: Why was the player shocked?

A: Because he was struck by lightning!

■

Q: When is it okay to make jokes about dying by volcano?

A: When the dust settles.

Q: What did one player say to his girlfriend who fell into a volcano?

A: "I *lava* you!"

Q: What pool is bad for swimming?

A: A lava pool!

∎

Q: What did the creeper say when he saw the volcano explode?

A: "Hsss, what a *lavaly* day!"

Q: Who's a volcano's favourite singer?
A: Johnny Ash!

■

Q: Why did the creeper and the ghast blast each other?
A: They had a falling out!

■

Q: What did the player call an adorable volcano?
A: *Lavable!*

■

Q: Why couldn't the hippie be saved from drowning?
A: He was too far out.

■

Q: What did the player say right after the volcano exploded?
A: "Unbe*lava*ble!"

■

Q: What did the player say right before he fell into a pool of lava?
A: "I'm going to go with the flow!"

First player: "What was the funniest time you were destroyed in Minecraft?"

Second player: "I was fleeing from a creeper and ran into another creeper!"

■

First player: "Can you recall the funniest way you were destroyed?"

Second player: "Water pushed me into lava!"

■

First player: "I'll always remember my friend's last word."

Second player: "What was it?"

First player: "Creeper!"

■

First player: "You know the saying, *He that fights and runs away, lives to fight another day*?"

Second player: "Yes, but in Minecraft, if you stay, fight, and die, you can always respawn!"

First player: "Did you hear about the player who ran straight into a cactus?"

Second player: "No, what happened?"

First player: "He got pins and needles!"

■

First player: "Did you hear about the player who was shocked while taking a selfie playing Minecraft?"

Second player: "Yes, but on the bright side, selfie sticks are also lightening rods!"

■

First player: "My cactus died!"

Second player: "Man, you are less nurturing than the desert!"

■

Q: Why did the player throw the chicken into the fire?

A: He wanted it barbecued.

TONGUE TWISTERS

David digs deep down and drowns!

Felicia and Francis fall furiously fast.

Falling Floyd flipped.

Digging diamonds, Dan drowned.

MINECRAFT LIMERICKS, POEMS, AND HAIKUS

There once was a player named Matt.
A stinky ghast pushed him into a vat.
Instead he caught a whiff,
Stumbled, and fell off a cliff.
Now, poor Matt went splat.

■

Roaring quite loudly,
Lava spilled every which way.
Now it is quiet.

■

Glittery diamonds
Sparkle in boiling lava.
Oops, I am drowning.

■

Diving in lava
Is never recommended
To retrieve diamonds.

■

The creeper was near.
I ran and fell off a cliff,
To avoid creepers!

■

So much disruption.
The volcano's eruption
And interruptions!

■

There once was a player named Jane.
Many gamers thought she was insane.
It was diamonds she spotted.
Oh, how she plotted.
Diving in lava caused her much pain.

■

There once was a player named Paul.
He killed nine creepers one brawl.
Nine's an excellent score,
Yet all he wanted was more!
But he lost, 'cause you can't win them all!

■

High up in the air he did sniff,
A rotting zombie—eww, what a whiff!
He felt sick to his stomach
And wanted to plummet,
So he jumped off a very big cliff.

■

There once was a player named Marie.

She ran from a creeper and scraped a knee.

He pushed her in lava.

She hit him with a guava.

She's lucky because she broke free!

RIDDLES, PUNS, AND MINECRAFT PHRASES

If one synchronized swimmer drowns in Minecraft, do the others drown, too?

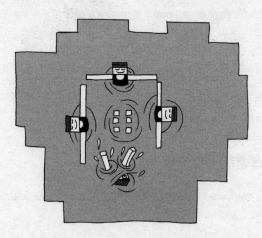

As long as I feed, I live. But when I drink, I die. What am I?
Fire.

I am used to transport lava. What am I?
A bucket.

I am evil. I start numerous forest fires. What am I?
Lava!

What did the volcano say to the two players having a conversation?
"I didn't mean to *inter-erupt*!"

DID YOU HEAR . . . ?

Did you hear about the player who tripped while carrying a
bucket of lava?
He was destroyed!

Did you hear about the player who accidentally shot himself with an arrow?
He was thankful that he could respawn!

Did you hear about the player who trapped himself in a wall?
He now knows to add doors.

Did you hear about the player who built a floor made of lava?
She's now hot-blooded!

Did you hear about the player who made a horde of ghasts upset?
There were a lot of tears shed!

Did you hear about the player who greeted an Enderman with a warm embrace?
She'll never make that mistake again!

Did you hear about the player who tried to irritate a bunch of slimes?
She's still trying to wash them off, but her skin is really smooth!

Did you hear about the creeper who didn't cross the road?
He was about to cross the road, then saw a player and exploded!

Did you hear about the player who tried to make an Ender Dragon a pet?
It was a noble attempt.

Did you hear about the player who asked the Enderman to be his best friend?
He decided he was better off on his own!

Did you hear about the player who rode a pig into a void?
We haven't heard from him since!

Did you hear about the player who dug straight down?
He didn't make it.

Did you hear about the player who built a beautiful home while it was freezing outside?
He made a lovely ice sculpture.

Did you hear about the player who told the witch her house was destroyed?
In turn, she destroyed him!

Did you hear about the player who blew himself up with TNT?
I'm sure you can guess what happened!

Did you hear about the player who thought he could fly in Survival mode?
He couldn't!

Did you hear about the player who walked in on two creepers?
He was destroyed!

Did you hear about the player who tried to farm in the Nether?
He was destroyed!

Did you hear about the player who tried to put a saddle on a creeper?
He went boom!

Did you hear about the player who was pushed into a ravine when water fell on him?
He made a big splash!

Did you hear about the player who was pushed off a cliff by a skeleton?
He respawned and told me about it!

Did you hear about the player who met a super creeper?
He was super destroyed!

Did you hear about the player who is out of this world?
He fell into a void!

Did you hear about the player who let a creeper do her hair?
She had a brush with death!

Did you hear about the player who kept a creeper as a pet?
He went boom.

Did you hear about the player who gorged himself on rotten meat?
He had a tummy ache!

Did you hear about the player who swam with squid?
He's eating calamari!

Did you know that if you jump off a twenty-four-block tower you can survive falling twenty-three blocks?
It's the twenty-fourth block that can hurt you!

Did you hear about the player who was swept up in tornado mod?
He was blown away!

CHAPTER 4

THE OVERWORLD

JOKES

Q: Why couldn't the Ender Dragon enter the Overworld?

A: Because he was past the portal of no return!

Q: Why are charged creepers always up-to-date?

A: Because they keep *current*!

Q: How do you know a dead charged creeper from a pile of healthy ones?

A: It's got no spark!

■

Q: What do charged creepers call a power failure?

A: A current event!

■

Q: How do charged creepers know when they fall in love?

A: They can feel the spark.

■

Q: What's grey and crispy and hangs from a tree?

A: An amateur charged creeper!

■

Q: What happened to the player who touched a charged creeper?

A: He got shocked!

■

Q: What did the zombie say when he ate a charged creeper?

A: "Shocking!"

Q: What would you call slimes that nibble on charged creepers?
A: *Electro-maggots.*

■

Q What do you call someone who touches a charged creeper?
A: Electrocuted!

■

Q: What hostile mob often winds up in jail?
A: Charged creepers!

■

Q: What's black and jumps up and down in a forest fire?
A: A burned player.

■

Q: What did the pig say in the desert?
A: "I'm *bacon* out here."

■

Q: If you are lost in the desert, is it better to ask for directions from villagers living in NPC villages or from snow golems?
A: Villagers, because snow golems in the desert are a mirage.

Q: Why didn't the player starve in the desert?

A: Because of all of the sand-*witches* there!

■

Q: What's a witch's favourite ballet?

A: *Swamp Lake*.

■

Q: Why did Steve go across the ocean?

A: To get to the other tide!

■

Q: What did the player say to the guardian when he was fleeing from the ocean?

A: "Sea ya later!"

■

Q: What did the ocean say to the shore?

A: Nothing, because oceans can't talk!

Q: What did the player get from the creeper who was struck by lightning?

A: A charge!

■

Q: What did the player say to the guardian?

A: "Let's not be *anemones*!"

■

Q: What washes up on tiny beaches?

A: Microwaves!

■

Q: Why did the cactus cross the road?

A: He was stuck to Steve!

Q: Why was the cactus sad?

A: No one would hug him!

■

Q: Why was the cactus messy?

A: A creeper exploded when it hugged it!

■

Q: Why was the player prickly?

A: He hugged a cactus.

■

Q: Why did the wolf point to the player when it saw a killer bunny?

A: He knew killer bunnies only attack wolves if players aren't around!

■

Q: How did the player thwart the killer bunny?

A: He named it Toast!

■

Q: Why is it hard to tell Minecraft witches apart?

A: Because you never know which witch is which!

Q: Why don't Minecraft witches fly on broomsticks?
A: They are afraid of flying off the handle!

■

Q: What is a witch's favourite school subject?
A: Spelling.

■

Q: Why did the player put name tags on the witches?
A: So he could tell which witch was which!

■

Q: What do witches eat?
A: Creepypasta!

■

Q: What noise does a witch's breakfast cereal make?
A: Snap, cackle, pop!

■

Q: What's a cold evil candle in Sweden called?
A: The wicked wick of the North!

Q: What did the player say to the witch he was battling?
A: "With any luck, you'll soon be well and get up for a spell."

■

Q: What's more dangerous than one angry witch?
A: Two angry witches!

■

Q: Why is a witch like a candle?
A: They're both wick-ed!

■

Q: What do you get when you put a witch in an icy biome?
A: A cold spell!

■

Q: What is a witch's favourite saying?
A: "We came, we saw, we conjured!"

■

Q: Why did the player attack the tiny slime?
A: She wanted a slimeball to make a brewing potion!

Q: What did the slime say to the player who pushed him off a cliff?

A: "I'll get you next *slime*!"

∎

Q: What sound does a witch make when she cries?

A: *Brew-hoo, brew-hoo.*

∎

Q: What do players call friendly witches?

A: Failures.

∎

Q: How did the player make the witch itch?

A: He took away her *w*.

First player: "I heard that the Plains are one of the biomes."

Second player: "Oh, yes, and do they have the Great Plains in Minecraft?"

First player: "No, the Great Plains are located at the great airport!"

■

First player: "I got lost in the Desert Biome."

Second player: "What were you *dune* out there?"

RIDDLES, PUNS, AND MINECRAFT PHRASES

It's a place where you spawn when you begin the game.
Where are you?
The Overworld.

I can jump, am adorable to look at, and you may think I'm tame. Who am I?
The killer rabbit!

If you tell a joke in the Forest Biome and nobody laughs, was it a joke?

It's where you start and spend most of your time.
Where are you?
In the Overworld.

I am millions of times larger than Earth and have many
different types of biomes. What am I?
The Overworld.

I can't enter the Overworld because there is no return portal.
Who am I?
An Ender Dragon.

MINECRAFT LIMERICKS, POEMS, AND HAIKUS

The creation of the killer bunny
Is actually quite funny.
Notch made a habit
Watching the killer rabbit
And was inspired by the havoc.

■

A crack and a flash of light
Turned the sky overwhelmingly bright.
My fear grew deeper,
Watching it charge a creeper.
I retreated, full of fright.

∎

Charged creepers explode
And emit a blue aura,
Destroying your world.

∎

Mooshrooms or mushrooms?
Yes, it's a bit confusing.
Think *moo*, then think cow!

∎

There once was a player named Susan.
Her goal was to clear up the confusion!
Food is a mushroom,
A cow is a mooshroom,
And that's her very bright conclusion!

∎

There once was a killer bunny,
Who was scary and not at all funny.
Hopping sixteen blocks, you see,
Run away, you must flee.
He wants blood and not your money!

■

No thorn enchantments.
They are totally useless
On killer rabbits.

■

In the Overworld,
Look in abandoned mineshafts
For sparkling diamonds!

■

There once was a player named Fred.
He tumbled and landed on his head.
In a mineshaft he fell,
Woke up and felt swell,
'Cause he found emeralds and a nice bed!

■

There once was a player named Merle
Who accidently threw an Ender pearl.
The result was endermites.
She fled from their deadly bites.
Oh, what a silly, sorry girl!

■

There once was a player named Dee.
She had the last laugh, you see.
Yes, she was slimed by a slime!
That was perfectly fine!
She used the goo for a potion of tea!

■

In the Overworld,
Grass blocks spawn naturally
And behave like dirt.

■

Endermites attack
Within sixteen blocks, I'm told.
Seventeen are safe!

■

His eyes are blood red
And he moves like a spider:
The killer bunny.

DID YOU KNOW . . . ?

Did you know there are three dimensions: Overworld, Nether, and End?

Did you know Nether portals in the Overworld can be used to teleport to the Nether?

Did you know that most mobs can spawn in the Overworld?

CHAPTER 5

JOCKEYS AND BABY ZOMBIE PIGMEN

JOKES

Q: **How did the player get the skeleton to jump off the spider?**

A: He jumped into water.

■

Q: **What's more disgusting than a baby zombie pigman eating a rabbit?**

A: A baby zombie pigman eating a whole cow!

■

Q: **What's funnier than a baby zombie pigman?**

A: A baby zombie pigman dressed up as Notch!

Q: **What did the mummy zombie pigman say to the baby zombie pigman?**

A: "You have your father's eyes . . . in your mouth!"

■

Q: **Who did the baby zombie pigman call after he lost his head?**

A: A headhunter!

■

Q: **What do polite baby zombie pigmen say when they first see you?**

A: "Pleased to eat you!"

■

First player: "Did you hear about the zombie pigman chicken jockey who kept an open mind?"

Second player: "No, what happened?"

First player: "His brains kept falling out!"

■

Q: **What did the zombie pigman chicken jockey say during the wrestling match?**

A: "Do you want a piece of me?"

Q. What did one spider jockey say to the other spider jockey?

A: Time flies when you're having flies!

■

Q: Why did the skeleton jump on the spider?

A: He wanted to take it for a spin.

■

Q: What do spider jockeys do when they get angry?

A: They go up the wall!

■

Q: Why was the player so calm when he saw the spider jockey on his keyboard?

A: It was under Ctrl.

■

Q: Why did the minecart accelerate?

A: Because the driver was a spider jockey!

Q: Why was the player acting so cool around the spider jockey?

A: It was daytime!

◼

Q: Why do spider jockeys hate winter?

A: Because the cold goes right through them.

◼

Q: What did the spider jockey say when he broke his new web?

A: Darn it!

◼

Q: Why was the wither skeleton jockey so calm?

A: Because nothing gets under his skin!

Q: Why did the wither skeleton jockey cross the road?

A: To get to the body shop!

■

Q: Who is a wither skeleton jockey's favourite _Star Trek_ character?

A: Bones.

■

Q: What did the player who spotted a wither skeleton jockey cross the road do?

A: She jumped out of her skin and joined him!

■

Q: What did the angry wither skeleton jockey call the player?

A: A bonehead!

■

Q: What do you call a crazy chicken jockey?

A: A cuckoo cluck.

Q: What type of cars would chicken jockeys drive?
A: Coupes!

■

Q: How do chicken jockeys slow dance?
A: Chick to chick!

■

Q: Why did the chicken jockey cross the road?
A: Because all the other chicken jockeys were doing it
and he wanted to fit in!

■

Q: Where do chicken jockeys come from?
A: Notch's imagination!

■

Q: What do you call a ghostly chicken jockey?
A: *Poultrygeist*!

■

Q: What did the chicken jockey get an award for?
A: *Deadication*!

Q: Why did the player find a disembodied head inside the piano?

A: A chicken jockey forgot it when he was playing by ear!

◾

Q: Why was the player afraid of the skeleton after he killed the spider?

A: He knew the skeleton would continue to attack.

Q: Why was the chicken jockey so good at defeating players?

A: He was quite *deadicated!*

■

Q: What should you do if a chicken jockey comes through your front door?

A: Run through your back door!

TONGUE TWISTERS

Spiders sometimes slither and spawn sideways.

Speedy spiders spun spiderwebs.

Wise spiders weave weaves wonderfully.

Seven silly spiders spin silky socks.

Carla's chicken chose carrots.

Robert rode 'round rumbling roads.

MINECRAFT LIMERICKS, POEMS, AND HAIKUS

A wither skeleton jockey,
His build was rather stocky.
He turned a player named Chuck
Into a very big puck.
He now enjoys playing hockey!

■

There once was a player named Snyder.
His eyes grew big as he spied her.
A skeleton of great height
Gave him a terrible fright!
'Cause he was riding a giant spider!

■

The spider jockey
Is elusive and deadly.
He will shoot and bite.

■

A baby zombie
Or baby zombie pigman
Will ride a chicken!

■

Who rides on its back:
A wither skeleton or
A plain skeleton?

■

Wither skeletons
Are tougher and scarier
Than plain skeletons!

■

Wither skeletons
Walk quite slowly when idle
And sprint, seeing you.

■

A chicken jockey
Despawns and will not lay eggs.
Yet, they can still breed.

Rare chicken jockeys
Are scary baby zombies
Riding a chicken.

■

Spider jockeys spawn
In tight, narrow enclosures.
Often suffocate!

RIDDLES, PUNS, AND MINECRAFT PHRASES

I have a 0.1 per cent chance of spawning. Who am I?
A chicken jockey!

I enjoy running around and I act a lot more like a zombie than a chicken. What am I?
A chicken jockey.

I am the most common jockey in Minecraft. Who am I?
A spider jockey.

I am the least common jockey. Who am I?
An Enderman jockey.

CHAPTER 6

SWORDS, POTIONS, AND BOWS AND ARROWS

JOKES

Q: What did the creeper say when he nearly got shot by a player's arrow?

A: "Wow; that was an *arrow* escape."

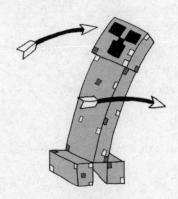

Q: How does Steve tie his shoes?

A: With a long bow!

■

Q: Why was the arrow angry?

A: Because his bow was cross!

■

Q: Why are sticks and string as deadly as sticks and stones?

A: Because with sticks and string you can craft bows!

■

Q: Why was the player shocked that her splash potion of harming didn't kill the skeleton?

A: Because skeletons are immune to splash potion!

■

Q: How did the player keep from getting hurt while battling a blaze?

A: He used a potion of fire resistance!

■

Q: What do you call a creeper in a pool of lava?

A: Destroyed!

Q: **What did the creeper say when he destroyed the player who took an invisibility potion?**

A: "Move along, nothing to see here."

■

Q: **How could the creeper tell that the invisible player was right in front of him?**

A: From his farts!

■

Q: **How are Minecraft players even more powerful than superheroes?**

A: Every day they survive several apocalypses!

■

Q: **Instead of taking an invisibility potion, how did the Minecraft player develop the power of becoming invisible?**

A: He turned invisible when no one was looking at him!

■

Q: **Why is leather armour the best for sneaking?**

A: It's made of *hide*!

Q: Why did the witch never get her enchantments right?
A: She kept on forgetting to use spellcheck!

■

First player: "Mines are fair and fatal to all players."
Second player: "How so?"
First player: "They are equal opportunity weapons."

■

First player: "I'm not a big fan of archery."
Second player: "Why?"
First player: "It has too many drawbacks."

■

First player: "You know the saying, 'The pen is mightier than the sword?'"
Second player: "Yes, what about it?"
First player: "Well, the person who said it never encountered an angry creeper with a sword!"

First player: "Please pass the salt."

Second player: "What for?"

First player: "So I can *a salt* with a deadly weapon."

■

First player: "I invited my brother to play Minecraft with me."

Second player: "How's it going?"

First player: "Great, he makes a good moving target!"

■

First player: "I have an archery joke."

Second player: "I'd love to hear it."

First player: "I'm not sure if it's quite on target. I could make one, but I don't really see the point."

■

Q: Why was everyone able to see the player who took the invisibility potion?

A: Because she forgot to take off her armour!

■

First player: "I went online and asked a site carrying Minecraft stuff if they had any they'd give me free."
Second player: "Did you get any?"
First player: "No, they blocked me!"

Q: Why couldn't the player hit the ghast?
A: Because his arrows were all *a quiver*.

First player: "I was in a play at school and I forgot my line."
Second player: "What did you do?"
First player: "I shouted 'Minecraft' because I wanted to say something constructive!"

MINECRAFT LIMERICKS, POEMS, AND HAIKUS

With hopes of creating a potion,
A player came up with a notion.
She took two instead of one.
Good news, no harm was done,
'Cause many potions resets one's motions!

■

Arrows on the ground
Will move, even if untouched,
Right toward the player!

■

Arrows catch fire
When shot through hot, hot lava,
but not through fire!

■

Arrows won't collide
If shot at Nether portals.
They often skip through.

■

Iron sword's texture
Came before the other swords.
Then more swords followed.

■

When blocking players,
Vertical moves speed remains,
Even if you fly.

■

Enchanted silk touch
Makes your sword collect cobwebs.
When using commands.

■

There once was a player named Mae.
Her arrows often did stray.
While shooting at creepers,
And missing their peepers,
Mae became the creepers' prey!

■

A player came up with a notion.
He created an enchanted potion.
His aim was to tame
Ender Dragons and seek fame.
Instead, he caused a commotion.

■

Careful where you aim.
Arrows will fly to the right.
Bows are off-centre.

■

There once was a player named Joe.
He loved shooting arrows with his bow.
He aimed at a ghast.
The arrows flew past.
One landed on his giant big toe!

■

An excellent maker of potions
Caused quite a bit of commotion
When he mixed up a quart
Of melon and Nether wart.
Bad tasting, he threw it in the ocean!

■

A player who lost all feeling,
Mixed up a potion of healing.
Ingredients she scanned.
Everything was at hand.
At last she's strong and appealing.

■

There once was a player named Nell.
At night she stumbled and fell.
She made a decision
To fix her night vision.
A potion has made her feel swell!

■

There once was a player named Trevor.
He was incredibly clever.
He caused a commotion
With a deadly potion.
Now hostile mobs fear him forever.

■

The potion made the zombie quake.
He stumbled and fell in a lake.
The player could bet
He wasn't dead yet,
Because he saw the zombie shake.

■

Mixing splash potions of harming
Can be incredibly alarming.
On some, it has no effect,
So you better elect
To find other ways of disarming!

■

Imagine Justin's giddy glee,
Turning fermented spider eye to tea!
Mixed with golden carrot
And adding Nether wart,
He's invisible and no one can see!

■

There once was a player named Jack.
One thing that he never did lack,
For he had a gift
and was incredibly swift.
With sugar and Nether wart, he made tracks!

■

Don't apply logic
When mixing new splash potions—
That's what Josh will say!

■

Hah! Trying to kill
Fierce Endermen and blazes—
Splash potions won't work.

RIDDLES, PUNS, AND MINECRAFT PHRASES

I can be made of wood, stone, gold, iron, and diamonds.
What am I?
Swords.

I can be crafted with leather, gold, fire, iron, and diamonds.
What am I?
Armour.

I bounce off minecarts and some mobs. What am I?
An arrow!

I am more powerful at breaking blocks than your fists.
What am I?
A sword!

You can't see me when I'm working. What am I?
A pen with an invisibility potion!

When I blow up and an arrow passes by, I can change the
arrow's direction. What am I?
TNT!

I help players hold their breath longer when they are underwater. What am I?
Water-breathing potion, which contains Nether wart and a raw pufferfish.

DID YOU HEAR . . . ?

Did you hear about the player who took the invisibility potion?
He was nothing to look at!

Did you hear about the player who tried to stick an arrow into the ground?
He couldn't see the point.

CHAPTER 7
SURVIVAL

JOKES

Q: Why is it bad to feed round bales of hay to Minecraft cows?

A: Because they won't get a square meal!

■

Q: What did the Minecraft player say after breaking rocks?

A: "I smashed it into total *obsidian*!"

■

Q: What did the polite Minecraft sheep named Elvis say after he was fed?

A: "Thank ewe very much!"

■

Q: Why did the Minecraft player label the rabbit?

A: He wanted a piece of toast.

Q: What do you get when you pour hot water down a rabbit hole?

A: Hot-cross bunnies.

■

Q: Why did the player run around the house?

A: She was running away from a creeper.

Q: What do you call a rude Minecraft cow?

A: Beef jerky.

■

Q: What's the best thing to put into pumpkin pie?

A: Your teeth!

Q: **When is a pumpkin not a pumpkin?**

A: When you drop it. Then, it's squash!

■

Q: **Do you know what a good Minecraft balanced diet is?**

A: A cookie in each hand!

■

Q: **Why couldn't the player reach the roof?**

A: He tried to climb up his house without a ladder!

■

Q: **Why couldn't the player run around?**

A: Because in Minecraft, nothing is round!

■

Q: **How did the player who ate raw chicken get rid of food poisoning?**

A: He drank milk!

■

Q: **Why did the player break the leaves of the oak tree?**

A: Because he was hungry and wanted to eat apples!

Q: **What do you get when you cross a cat with a squid?**
A: *Cat-amari*!

■

Q: **How does an apple a day keep the ghast away?**
A: When you take perfect aim!

■

Q: **How do you make an apple puff?**
A: Chase it around your garden!

■

Q: **How do you hide an Ender Dragon?**
A: Paint his toenails red and put him in an apple orchard!

■

Q: **What kind of keys do players like to carry?**
A: Cookies!

■

Q: **What is blue and purple and crawls through a field?**
A: Steve looking for his lost cookies!

Q: Why did Steve only bake one cookie?
A: Because he ate the rest of the dough!

■

Q: How did the Minecraft player make the stew richer?
A: He added fourteen carrots!

■

Q: What did the players get when they played tug-of-war with a pig?
A: Pulled pork!

■

Q: What did one player say when he swiped the cake from his opponent?
A: "That was a piece of cake!"

■

Q: How do Minecraft witches style their hair?
A: With scare spray!

■

Q: How do you make your meals richer?
A: Add karats!

Q: What's invisible and smells like carrots?
A: Bunny farts!

■

Q: How did the Minecraft player communicate with fish?
A: He dropped a line.

■

Q: How does a creeper say hello?
A: *"Kaboom!"*

■

Q: Why did the witch stand up in front of the other witches?
A: Because she had to give a *screech*.

■

Q: If there was a national anthem for Minecraft, what
would it be?
A: "I Will Survive!"

Q: How is a Minecraft player like a person meditating?

A: When they eat, both say, "Om!"

■

Q: Why are carrots thin and pointy?

A: Because if they were round, they wouldn't be in Minecraft.

■

Q: What do you get when you cross a fishing rod with a player's dirty sock?

A: A hook, line, and stinker!

■

Q: Why did the zombie pigman go to the dentist?

A: To improve his bite.

■

Q: How did the player get hold of a potato?

A: He killed a zombie!

■

Q: What do you call a potato that you steal from a zombie?

A: A hot potato!

Q: What did the player call a baby potato?
A: Small fry!

■

Q: Which way did the player carrying a bunch of potatoes travel?
A: He took the fork in the road!

■

Q: What does Taylor Swift sing when she plays Minecraft and eats potatoes?
A: "Taters gonna tate!"

■

Q: What's the difference between potatoes and zombies?
A: You can't mash zombies!

■

Q: What do you get when you cross a potato with a hostile mob?
A: Mashed potatoes!

■

Q: How does Jamie Oliver make the best pickles?
A: He uses Herobrine!

Q: Who was the guest of honour at the Brine family reunion?
A: Herobrine!

■

Q: What did one player say to the other who wasn't doing a good job flying?
A: "That's not flying; that's falling!"

■

First player: "Did you know that take-offs are optional?"
Second player: "Yes, and landing is mandatory!"

■

First player: "Did you know flying isn't dangerous?"
Second player: "Of course! *Crashing* is dangerous!"

■

Q: Who does Superman look up to?
A: Herobrine!

First player: "Most people would think that flying is the greatest thrill."

Second player: "It's not?"

First player: "Nope. It's landing!"

■

First player: "If you build it, they will come!"

Second player: "Yes, but that means creepers, ghasts, and other hostile mobs, too!"

■

First player: "My friends and I were so nervous constructing our first Minecraft tower."

Second player: "I know. The buildup was intense!"

■

First player: "Vegetables are a must on my diet!"

Second player: "Mine, too. I suggest we start with pumpkin pie!"

■

First player: "Do you like baked apples?"

Second player: "Yes, I do. Why?"

First player: "That's good, because your orchard's on fire."

First player: "Did you hear about the apple that the creeper threw that stopped in mid-air?"

Second player: "No, what happened?"

First player: "It ran out of juice!"

■

First player: "If it took six pigs two hours to eat carrots in the field, how many hours would it take three pigs?"

Second player: "None, because the six pigs would have eaten all of them!"

■

First player: "What is the left side of an apple?"

Second player: "The side that you don't eat!"

■

First player: "How do you make an apple turnover?"

Second player: "You push it down a hill."

■

First player: "I upgraded my armour."

Second player: "How'd you do that?"

First player: "They were having a sale for one *knight* only!"

Knock, knock
Who's there?
You're a diamond?
You're a diamond who?
You're a *diamond* me crazy!

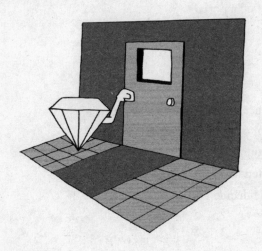

Knock, knock.
Who's there?
Carrot.
Carrot, who?
Do you *carrot* all about me?

MINECRAFT LIMERICKS, POEMS, AND HAIKUS

There once was a player named Faye.
Wandering off the path, she did stray.
She opened a portal
And met an immortal.
Now, Faye is not doing okay!

■

There once was a builder named Marie,
She went on a building spree.
She encountered some creepers,
Who acted like grim reapers,
So Marie decided to flee.

■

It might sound creepy, so you say,
That I spend time killing zombies each day.
It's not a profession.
It's more like an obsession.
That's why I play all night and all day!

■

There once was a player named Alice.
Sometimes she was quite callous.
Her stomach was tough.
The puffer she ate was rough.
Now poor Alice was filled with malice!

■

The ghast, he started to cry
When the player asked him, "Why?"
He answered, "The food
Is tasteless and crude."
He would have preferred pumpkin pie!

■

A village butcher
Will trade seven cooked pork chops
For an emerald.

■

Clownfish taste funny.
Players will eat them uncooked.
It is like sushi.

■

Throw back the puffer.
Eating it will poison you
And make you hungry.

■

You make mushroom stew
By milking mooshrooms with bowls.
Then you eat, om nom!

■

Tame, breed, grow, and heal
Horses with golden carrots.
Bunnies like them, too!

■

It's not at all true
That golden carrot potions
Can cure night vision.

RIDDLES, PUNS, AND MINECRAFT PHRASES

I am made of diamonds, obsidian, and a book. What am I?
An enchantment table.

I spawn underground. What am I?
A mineshaft.

The more you take from it, the larger it gets. What am I?
A ditch.

I move silently without wings, and I hang on strong strings.
What am I?
A spider.

First you see me in the grass dressed in yellow. When I'm a
dainty white, I fly away. What am I?
A dandelion.

I am quite nutritious if you cook me in a furnace. What am I?
A cod.

I'm very tempting to eat, and my skin is red. What am I?
An apple.

You will become hungry after eating me. What am I?
A pufferfish.

I must die so you can live. What am I?
An animal that drops food.

Why do we bake cookies and cook bacon?

The player who stole my cookie really took the biscuit!

What food restores some of your hunger and at the same
time depletes your hunger meter at a faster rate?
Rotting flesh!

CHAPTER 8

CREATIVE

JOKES

Q: What is Steve and Alex's favourite song?

A: "We Built This City."

■

Q: Why did the player bring gold and silver into his boat?

A: He needed ores!

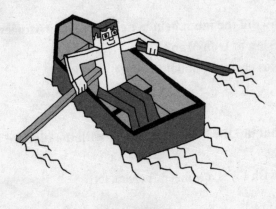

Q: **Why did Steve's white shirt turn blue?**

A: Because he washed it with lapis in the pockets!

■

Q: **What's the difference between a good landing and a great landing?**

A: In Minecraft a good landing is where you can walk away, and a great landing is when you have no injuries!

■

Q: **How do you measure a Minecraft player's shoe size?**

A: In square feet.

■

Q: **Why did the mum help her child create a Minecraft version of Iron Man?**

A: It was character building.

■

Q: **What did the Minecraft player with the blocked nose say?**

A: "I wish I was a Minecraft character!"

Q: How do Minecraft players stay calm?

A: They take a walk around the block!

∎

Q: What happened to the player who was hit by a piano?

A: He became *A-flat minor*!

Q: What's the tallest building in Minecraft?

A: The library, because it has the most stories!

∎

Q: Why was the player barking up the wrong tree?

A: Because he was *stumped* that it *wooden* give him wood!

First player: "My login password is CreeperGhastSteveandAlex."
Second player: "Why is it so long?"
First player: "It has to have at least four characters."

■

Knock, knock,
Who's there?
Theodore.
Theodore who?
Theodore was open, so I'm coming in!

■

Q: What did the player say while rolling down a bumpy road?

A: "I can feel my *cart* pounding!"

MINECRAFT LIMERICKS, POEMS, AND HAIKUS

There once was a player named Roy.
He loved to build and destroy
With much creativity
And productivity,
Which, in creative, he would employ!

■

A player was exploring a cave.
He had a very close shave.
He stepped on a cave spider,
Who was a great fighter.
Fortunately, he was faster than brave!

■

There once was a player named Lou.
His dream was to build a big zoo.
He filled it with pigs and sheep,
And even creepers that creep—
Playing Minecraft, he knew just what to do!

■

A player named Katie was quite skilled.
She knew what she wanted to build:
A castle so high
That would reach the sky.
Now her dream was completely fulfilled.

∎

There one was player named Joan.
She dreamed of building a home.
A great imagination,
She crafted a sensation
That she created all on her own!

∎

Creative allows
All players to destroy blocks.
You can also fly.

∎

Falling through a hole
Happens in bedrock layer
In Creative mode.

∎

Tap the space bar twice
So you fly up near the top.
Shift makes you go down.

■

In Creative mode,
Just be careful not to fall
Into the dark void.

■

Flying above clouds,
You can see the sun and moon.
Both are visible.

■

Flying high enough,
You can spot the sun and moon
When looking downward!

RIDDLES, PUNS, AND MINECRAFT PHRASES

Always remember to keep the number of landings you make equal to the number of take-offs you've made!

When flying, always remember that good judgement comes from experience. Unfortunately, experience comes from bad judgement!

I sleep all day and fly by night. I have no feathers. What am I?
A bat.

There's no hunger or ill health. Where am I?
In Creative mode!

I am optional and mandatory. What am I?
Take-offs and landings!

I can be used to free up large outdoor areas and get rid of grass. What am I?
A bucket of water!

I can slow you down and make a good trap for hostile mobs.
What am I?
Soul sand.

I am a good tool for building underwater and preventing
leaks. What am I?
A ladder!

You can carry all of your food, but you can't eat it here.
Where are you?
Creative mode!

You are out of blocks and can still build with me. What am I?
The side of a torch!

I will help you breathe underwater. What am I?
A torch.

DID YOU KNOW . . . ?

Did you know you can have unlimited items in Creative mode?

Did you know you can fly in Creative mode?

Did you know that, in Creative mode, you can't die unless you fall into the void?

Did you know that, in the Pocket Edition, if you die in Creative mode, you get to keep your entire inventory?

Did you know that torches create temporary air pockets underwater?

Did you know that torches can break stacks of sand and gravel?

Did you know that you can use a torch to hold up sand and gravel?

Did you know that ladders and signs can stop water and lava from flowing?

Did you know that blazes hate snowballs?

Did you know that soul sand can make you sink?

Did you know that just two buckets of water will give you an infinite supply of water?

CHAPTER 9

PEACEFUL TO THE END

JOKES

Q: Why couldn't the hostile mob spawn?

A: Because he was in Peaceful mode.

■

Q: What do you call a cow that works on a Minecraft player's yard?

A: A lawn *moo-er*.

■

Q: Why was the Old West gunfighter such a fan of Minecraft?

A: He liked to put a notch in his six shooter!

Q: What did one witch say to the other?

A: "Your potion *blew* me away!"

■

Q: What did the player say to the Ender Dragon?

A: "You want a *peace* of me?"

■

Q: What did the competitive Minecraft coach say to his youngest player?

A: "There's no crying in Minecraft."

Q: What did President Obama say the first time he played Minecraft?

A: Who knows? The press never covers the really important stuff.

■

Q: What's a Minecraft player's favourite car?

A: The Nissan Cube!

■

Q: What can make a Minecraft player cry?

A: Nothing. We're really tough!

■

Q: What did the zombie see when he pulled down the Enderman's trousers?

A: *Ender*pants!

Q: What can make a Minecraft player cry?

A: Everything. We're really sensitive!

■

Q: What did the player call the deaf Ender Dragon?

A: Anything he wanted, because the Ender Dragon couldn't hear him!

■

Q: What do you get when an Ender Dragon sneezes?

A: Out of the way!

■

Q: Where do you go when an Ender Dragon farts?

A: Far, far away!

■

Q: Why did the Ender Dragon cross the road?

A: Because chickens weren't invented yet!

■

Q: What powers do Minecraft players have?

A: Incredible ones, because they keep on surviving the End!

Q: Why can't Minecraft players spell Armageddon?
A: Because it's not the End!

■

Q: What song will players sing at the End?
A: "It's the End of the World."

■

First player: "I want to start in Hardcore mode."
Second player: "All I am saying is give *peace* a chance!"

First player: "What song lyrics do Minecraft players like to sing?"

Second player: "And now the End is here, and I have faced my final battle, and did it Notch's way!"

■

First player: "I heard the End has its own soundtrack."

Second player: "What does it sound like?"

First player: "You can only hear it in the End."

MINECRAFT LIMERICKS, POEMS, AND HAIKUS

John started off in Peaceful mode.

He built a very grand abode.

No fears from hostile creatures—

This mode it didn't feature,

Except one Ender Dragon on this road.

■

A player went up to the next level.

He thought he encountered the devil.

Please, don't be so daft!

There's no devil in Minecraft.

Just a ghast, which is on the same level!

■

There once was a player named Shirl.

She found an Ender pearl.

She dreamed of transporting

And thought it was very sporting.

She threw it and gave it a whirl!

■

There once was a player named Al.

He was everyone's favourite pal.

He tamed an Ender Dragon,

Who now drives his wagon,

And the dragon lives in Al's corral!

■

Want to teleport?
You should throw an Ender pearl
And you will arrive!

■

Hostile mobs can spawn
And create lots of damage.
This is quite normal.

■

When difficulty
Is set to Peaceful level,
Hostile mobs won't spawn.

■

Ender pearls that fall
Into the void won't trigger
You to teleport.

■

A stark empty plane;
A floating planet island.
It is called the End.

■

Lava flows faster,
It's just like in the Nether,
Only in the End.

■

An endless, dark sky,
With a huge mass of end stone,
Looks like a deep void.

■

You'll find small islands
And obsidian pillars
Scattered in the End!

■

Exploding beds start
Fires and portals won't work
When you reach the End.

RIDDLES AND PUNS

My poison is useless in easy mode. Who am I?
A cave spider.

I flow faster in the End and in the Nether. What am I?
Lava.

At night they appear without being fetched. By day they are
gone without being stolen. What are they?
Stars.

When I break, I sound just like shattered glass. What am I?
An End portal frame.

When I am slain, I drop one Ender pearl. Who am I?
An Enderman.

I have a 5 per cent chance of spawning endermites. What am I?
An Ender pearl.

Villagers no longer use me and I craft the eyes. What am I?
Ender pearls.

The day to night cycle doesn't exist. Where are you?
At the End!

All of the crystals are destroyed and I am powerless. Who am I?
The Ender Dragon.

How can you create an exit portal from the End?
Destroy the Ender Dragon.

Clocks and compasses spin randomly and if you try to sleep
in a bed it will explode. Where are you?
The End!

DID YOU KNOW . . . ?

Did you know that if you ride a minecart into an active End portal, it won't take you to the End?

Did you know that if you exit that cart, you will be sent to the End?

Did you know that if you destroy the frame, the portal will still work?

Did you know that if you spawn an Ender Dragon outside of the End, the dragon will drop an exit portal, taking you to the End?

Did you know that if you want to find the End, the first thing you need to do is first find and then complete an End portal?

CHAPTER 10

RESPAWNING

JOKES

Q: Why did the Minecraft player continue to play football with a broken leg?

A: He was waiting to respawn.

■

Q: Why didn't the Minecraft player immediately text back her friend?

A: She was waiting to respawn!

■

Q: What did the player say when he saw the same creeper who recently destroyed him?

A: "You are a blast from the past!"

Q: **Why will the world never end?**

A: Because Minecraft players keep on respawning.

■

Q: **What did the Minecraft player wish for?**

A: To respawn as Steve!

■

Q: **What type of circle do Minecraft players love?**

A: The circle of life!

■

Q: **What happened to the player who became totally absorbed with Minecraft?**

A: He entered *nerdvana*!

■

Q: **What did the Minecraft player say to the player who died for the first time?**

A: "I didn't believe in respawning at first, either!"

■

Q: **What's a Minecraft player's favourite song?**

A: "Karma Chameleon," because players keep on coming and going.

Q: What are the two things Minecraft players can count on?

A: Destruction and respawning!

■

Q: What happens right before witches respawn?

A: They go away for a spell!

■

Q: What did the Minecraft player say right before he was destroyed?

A: "I'll be right back!"

■

Q: What did the respawned player say?

A: "Did and done that before!"

■

Q: What is a respawned player's favourite song lyrics?

A: "A whole new world."

■

Q: What did one player say to the other?

A: "I've heard respawning is making a comeback!"

Q: What is the most popular phrase in Minecraft?
A: "You died!"

■

Q: What's the difference between a cat and a Minecraft player?
A: A cat only has nine lives!

■

Q: What did the ghast say to the player who died and respawned?
A: "Déjà Boo!"

■

Q: Why did the player wish he could take his math test in Minecraft?
A: Because if he failed, he could retake!

■

Q: How do you keep a monster from respawning?
A: Stick a name tag on him.

■

Q: What did the creeper say to the respawned player?
A: "I think we've met before!"

Q: What film don't Minecraft players get?

A: The James Bond film, *You Only Live Twice*.

■

Q: How is Minecraft like déjà vu?

A: Every time you play the game, you feel like you've been here before.

■

Q: What song lyrics do Minecraft players like to sing?

A: "We have all been here before!"

■

Q: What is a Minecraft player's worst nightmare?

A: Losing the ability to respawn!

■

First player: "Why did the player feel immortal?"

Second player: "I don't know, why?"

First player: "Because Minecraft gamers keep on respawning!"

■

First player: "If a player was born in Sweden, raised in America, and died in Mexico, what does that make him?"
Second player: "Deceased."

■

First player: "What do you eat before you die?"
Second player: "You bite the dust!"

■

First player: "I had a near death experience."
Second player: "What happened?"
First player: "I escaped from a zombie attack and then saw Notch!"

■

First player: "Have you heard the jokes about immortality?"
Second player: "No, I haven't."
First player: "That's too bad. They never get old!"

■

First player: "I found something round in Minecraft!"
Second player: "You did? What?"
First player: "A circle of life!"

■

First player: "There's a first time for everything . . ."
Second player: "Except when you respawn!"

■

First player: "Studies show that for every fifteen minutes you laugh, you gain an extra day of life."
Second player: "That's nothing. In Minecraft, we respawn every time we are destroyed!"

■

First player: "Time is a great healer."
Second player: "That's true, but in Minecraft, you keep on respawning!"

MINECRAFT LIMERICKS, POEMS, AND HAIKUS

There once was a player named Lou.
This land seems familiar, it's true!
He felt pretty sure
He had been here before.
This is what's called déjà vu!

■

The player with an old computer,
Couldn't plug in her new router;
It wouldn't unlock
And gave her a shock.
She died, and I had to reboot her!

■

The Minecraft player had died.
In her gaming skills, she took deep pride.
Happy and reborn,
This she soon had sworn:
"I'll learn from my mistakes!" she cried.

■

There once was player named Belle.
While battling ghasts, she fell.
But while falling she gave a yawn.
She knew she would respawn.
And in her new skin, she felt swell.

■

She lost a battle
And fell straight down with a splat!
Don't fret; she respawned.

■

When life is quite bad,
All we really have to do
Is stop and reboot!

RIDDLES, PUNS, AND MINECRAFT PHRASES

Why do Minecraft players like the number thirty-two? Because hostile mobs cease to exist if you are within thirty-two blocks of them for more than thirty seconds!

Best excuse ever: "I didn't call you back because I was waiting to respawn!"

The player was so sure he would respawn that he wrote a will leaving everything to himself!

You know you've been playing Minecraft too long when your hands start to bleed and you can't figure out why you haven't respawned.

There's a first time for everything, except as a Minecraft player respawning!

After being destroyed again, the Minecraft player said, BRB (Be Right Back) instead of RIP.

Can Minecraft players get déjà vu?

Respawning isn't like amnesia. You remember and keep on getting better!

If at first you don't succeed, respawn, respawn again!

Respawning is so fun that you keep on doing it over and over again!

Keep calm and respawn!

Great players don't really die. They keep on respawning!

By respawning, we learn from our mistakes!

CHAPTER 11

YOU MIGHT BE A MINECRAFT ADDICT IF . . .

You might be a Minecraft addict if your friends and family call you a blockhead and you don't mind.

You might be a Minecraft addict if you try to make things out of cubed carrots.

You might be a Minecraft addict if you punch trees to gather wood for your fireplace.

You might be a Minecraft addict if you scour gravel driveways in search of flint.

You might be a Minecraft addict if you put sand in the oven hoping it will turn into glass.

You might be a Minecraft addict if you argue with your science teacher who says trees really do have roots and branches.

You might be a Minecraft addict if you sleep in Minecraft when you are tired in real life.

You might be a Minecraft addict if you go outside in the snow dressed in just a T-shirt and trousers.

You might be a Minecraft addict if you get upset that the tree you planted in your backyard takes months to grow.

You might be a Minecraft addict if you arrange your school supplies in groups of sixty-four.

You might be a Minecraft addict if you've built tunnels under your home looking for coal and iron.

You might be a Minecraft addict if you get coal for your birthday and think it's a great gift.

You might be a Minecraft addict if you know more about the game than about your school work.

You might be a Minecraft addict if you've taken up cactus gardening and you don't live in a dry biome.

You might be a Minecraft addict if you start digging for glowstone to save energy.

You might be a Minecraft addict if you write Minecraft fan fiction for your English homework.

You might be a Minecraft addict if you've read and critiqued other Minecraft players' fan fiction.

You might be a Minecraft addict if your wardrobe consists of simple T-shirts and purple trousers.

You might be a Minecraft addict if you can't understand why your farm doesn't tend to itself.

You might be a Minecraft addict if all four walls in your room have at least one picture of Steve and Alex.

You might be a Minecraft addict if you add a trap door in your room to hide from invading creepers.

You might be a Minecraft addict if you don't own anything that is round.

You might be a Minecraft addict if you petition your school to add Swedish as a language requirement.

You might be a Minecraft addict if you study Swedish with the goal of getting updates faster.

You might be a Minecraft addict if you only listen to Minecraft music on your iPod.

You might be a Minecraft addict if you watch YouTube Minecraft videos hourly.

You might be a Minecraft addict if you tell your friends and everyone you meet that they can build anything.

You might be a Minecraft addict if all your clocks just show when dusk and dawn happen.

You might be a Minecraft addict if your greatest ambition is to be Steve.

You might be a Minecraft addict if you start building a watch that just says "dusk" and "dawn."

You might be a Minecraft addict if you argue with a farmer that wool comes from punching sheep.

You might be a Minecraft addict if you sit too close to the screen and your eyes are now square.

You might be a Minecraft addict if you get nostalgic about Indev.

You might be a Minecraft addict if you get confused when you see a ball roll.

You might be a Minecraft addict if you spend hours searching for Herobrine.

You might be a Minecraft addict if you spend every waking moment thinking about Minecraft.

You might be a Minecraft addict if you dream in pixels.

You might be a Minecraft addict if you mistake your dog for a sheep.

You might be a Minecraft addict if you go on holiday to the beach and spend all of your time punching the sand.

You might be a Minecraft addict if you picture everything in blocks and pixels.

You might be a Minecraft addict if you decorate your room by stacking everything into blocks.

You might be a Minecraft addict if you refuse to make eye contact with tall people dressed in black.

You might be a Minecraft addict if your mum tells you to tidy your room and instead you tidy up the house you just created.

You might be a Minecraft addict if you forget to give your mum a present for her birthday and instead get her a Minecraft account XD.

You might be a Minecraft addict if you wake up on a real aeroplane, look out the window, and are convinced you are looking at a world hole.

You might be a Minecraft addict if you get confused when your friends talk about other things to do on a computer.

You might be a Minecraft addict if you are home alone and turn on all of the lights because you are convinced that creepers spawn in real life!

You might be a Minecraft addict if you think the world is square.

You might be a Minecraft addict if you have a shrine to Notch in your room.

You might be a Minecraft addict if you go to a farm and are confused why the sheep, pigs, and horses aren't square.

You might be a Minecraft addict if you hear the words: block, mine, coal, bedrock, craft, biome, village, or survival, and immediately think of Minecraft.

You might be a Minecraft addict if you meet a guy named Steve and ask him if he's related to the *real* Steve.

You might be a Minecraft addict if you believe you are a world traveller because of the places you've built.

You might be a Minecraft addict if you hear a *boom* outside your window and think it's a creeper.

You might be a Minecraft addict if you sleep with the lights on because you are afraid of creepers.

You might be a Minecraft addict if you wake up in the middle of the night and want to light a torch.

You might be a Minecraft addict if you hear a *sssssss* coming from the TV and you run to get your bow and arrow.

You might be a Minecraft addict if you get a high score at the Minecraft Addiction test site.

You might be a Minecraft addict if you place torches everywhere around your house so nothing spawns in it.

You might be a Minecraft addict if you place a plank of wood at your front door, thinking it will open as soon as you step on it.

You might be a Minecraft addict if you buy only fifteen feet of wire because you think it will lose power after fifteen feet.

You might be a Minecraft addict if you look at a brick building and think, *Man, that's a lot of clay!*

You might be a Minecraft addict if you go to a farm and try to saddle a pig so you can ride it.

You might be a Minecraft addict if you try to make your own water supply by putting one bucket of water at each end of a hole you dug.

You might be a Minecraft addict if you broke your glasses and thought, *Oh no, what texture pack is this?*

You might be a Minecraft addict if you throw a snowball at a sheep and expect wool or a clock to drop.

You might be a Minecraft addict if your best friend is wearing a great outfit and you ask her where she bought that nice skin.

You might be a Minecraft addict if you admire your friend's skin and ask her where she crafted it.

You might be a Minecraft addict if you look at pictures of faraway places and think, *I can build a nice base there!*

You might be a Minecraft addict if you look at buildings and think how you can craft them.

You might be a Minecraft addict if you dress up in iron trousers and don't understand why they are so uncomfortable.

You might be a Minecraft addict if you ask your parents to get you a slime for a pet.

You might be a Minecraft addict if you check the distance to the floor so you don't fall.

You might be a Minecraft addict if you see the sun start to set and you gather sticks to look for coal.

You might be a Minecraft addict if you mould your mashed potatoes into cubes.

You might be a Minecraft addict if you think Pong is a gateway game.

You might be a Minecraft addict if you only play for six hours straight because you are cutting back.

You might be a Minecraft addict if you realize that you've built more buildings than all of the buildings in your town.

You might be a Minecraft addict if you create block-themed holiday decorations.

You might be a Minecraft addict if you're drowning and think you'll respawn.

You might be a Minecraft addict if you hear a noise in the middle of the night and think, *It's okay, I have Peaceful mode on!*

You might be a Minecraft addict if you wonder, *Does this diamond armour make me look too square?*

You might be a Minecraft addict if instead of turning the handle to open the door, you smash it with a pickaxe.

You might be a Minecraft addict if you cut out the middle of a tree and are surprised when it falls.

You might be a Minecraft addict if you get confused by round shapes.

You might be a Minecraft addict if you spill something and put a sign next to it to stop it from spreading.

You might be a Minecraft addict if you throw eggs on the ground and expect to see a chicken.

You might be a Minecraft addict if the kettle whistles and you think, *Creeper!*

You might be a Minecraft addict if you drive a boat to the bottom of a waterfall and expect it to be rocketed to the top.

You might be a Minecraft addict if you don't understand why you can't carry all of the groceries in one trip.

You might be a Minecraft addict if you are afraid of pigs because you think one day they will transform into zombie pigmen.

You might be a Minecraft addict if you visit a farm and are surprised that there are no pink or yellow sheep.

You might be a Minecraft addict if you try on new clothes and think, *This* skin *looks great on me!*

You might be a Minecraft addict if you see mossy stone and think it's a dungeon.

You might be a Minecraft addict if you smack snow with a shovel and expect snowballs to pop up.

You might be a Minecraft addict if you hear someone go "Urg" and you ask your friend if he's packing a sword so you can kill a zombie.

You might be a Minecraft addict if you see a sign stating WE BUY GOLD and think, *No way, I'm saving my gold for power rails.*

You might be a Minecraft addict if you see a circle and think, *That's not right.*

You might be a Minecraft addict if you can't think outside the blocks.

You might be a Minecraft addict if you seriously think about becoming an actual miner when you grow up.

You might be a Minecraft addict if you do a double take because you thought you saw a creeper following you, but it turned out to be your little sister.

You might be a Minecraft addict if you hear someone groan and you shout, "Zombie!"

You might be a Minecraft addict if you hear a dog bark and think if you follow the sound, you'll find a pack of wolves.

You might be a Minecraft addict if you ask your mum to replace the light in your room with a torch.

You might be a Minecraft addict if you run away when your cat hisses because you think you heard a creeper.

You might be a Minecraft addict if you spot a water fountain and wish you had a bucket on you.

You might be a Minecraft addict if you signed up for art classes just so you could spend your time sketching stuff to build later.

You might be a Minecraft addict if you're young and look forward to turning sixty-four.

You might be a Minecraft addict if someone asks you how big your house is and you answer, "Four chunks!"

You might be a Minecraft addict if you don't understand why your dog doesn't sit when you right click.

You might be a Minecraft addict if you see a spider and are puzzled that it's not as big as you.

You might be a Minecraft addict if you are terrified of thunderstorms because you believe hostile mobs will spawn.

You might be a Minecraft addict if you knew that the game was originally called *Cave Game*.

You might be a Minecraft addict if you knew the creeper started as a coding error.

You might be a Minecraft addict if you put cocoa beans on the kitchen counter, pour milk on them, and expect to make chocolate milk.

You might be a Minecraft addict if you tried to convince your family to move to Stockholm so you could attend the school where Minecraft was made a compulsory part of the curriculum.

You might be a Minecraft addict if you can't read normal clocks.

You might be a Minecraft addict if you look at your pet and think, *Notch has made a new mob!*

You might be a Minecraft addict if your favourite pastime is going to the junkyard to watch them crush cars into cubes.

CHAPTER 12

MINECRAFT SAYINGS WE'D LIKE TO SEE

- Never dig down!

- Ssss! Boom!

- Live life to the fullest. Take it up a Notch!

- Just one more block!

- Another creeper bites the dust!

- If you build it, hostile mobs will come!

- Live in your world. Play in mines!

- If you can mine it, you can craft it!

- WWND?

- To be ore not to be?

- Follow me to Nether Nether land.

- We holiday in the Netherlands.

- Ender the Dragon!

- Herobrine the Legend!

- Never hug a creeper!

- I lava you!

- I'd rather be mining!

- A golden apple a day keeps the doctor away!

- Take it up a Notch!

- Minecraft: it's LEGO with zombies!

- Minecraft: what a ghast!

- Minecraft: can you dig it?

- Minecraft: Sandpit 2.0!

- I did Minecraft!

- Give a wolf a bone!

- I'm in a feud with the mob!

- Veni, Vidi, Vici, Minecraft!

- Love is never having to explain Minecraft!

- It's simply Minecraft over matter!

- Minecraft is like a box of chocolates: you never know what's going to get you!

- There's always time for Minecraft!

- Minecraft: think inside and outside the blocks!

- Minecraft: no limit to your imagination!

- I came, I saw, I mined!

- Victory is Mine . . . craft!

- Minecraft: where inspiration never sleeps and Nether do you!

- Success: it's a Mine . . . craft game!

- Herobrine: now you see him, now you don't!

- Minecraft: there is no substitute!

- Minecraft: just play it!

- I ain't afraid of no ghasts!

- Minecraft: where everything is possible!

- Keep on playing those Minecraft games forever!

- Minecraft: think blocks!

- Minecraft: build it your way!

- Minecraft: be here now!

- If you build it, creepers will come!

- Minecraft: nothing ventured, nothing gamed.

- The only thing we have to fear are creepers and other hostile mobs!

- You don't know what you can do until you start building.

- The cavern you choose to enter may be filled with lava!

- Do no harm, unless you encounter creepers and other hostile mobs!

- No regrets, because you can respawn!

- Never underestimate the power of your Mine . . . craft!

- If you think it, you can build it.

- Minecraft: yes, you can!

- I see Herobrine!

- Minecraft: I'll be back!

- May the blocks be with you!

- Minecraft: to the Nether and beyond!

- I have a feeling we're not in the Nether anymore!

- Minecraft: another block in the wall!

- In the end, you know it's all blocks.

- "Mr. Steve, tear down this wall!"

- Gravity is a lifestyle choice.

- It's a big world. Someone has to explore it!

- I mine, therefore I craft!

- One player's hut is another player's castle!

- There's no place like the mines!

- Minecraft: doing the same thing over and over again and expecting different results.

- The best things in life are blocks.

- Be the miner and shape the world!

- Those who matter mine, and those who mine matter!

- When life gives you creepers . . . run!

- Keep calm and mine!

- Minecraft the Movie, Episode 1: The Dark Mine Rises!

- Minecraft the Movie, Episode 2: A Good Day to Mine Hard!

- I'm one step closer to diamonds!

- How to train your Ender Dragon!

- Minecraft the Movie, Episode 3: The Iron Golem Giant!

- Minecraft the Movie, Episode 4: Wreck-it Steve!

MINECRAFT SAYINGS WE'D LIKE TO SEE

- Mine, create, survive!

- Minecraft: building a better world today and tomorrow!

- We are here to create!

- Don't mess with the creeper!

- Those diamonds won't mine themselves!

- Miners don't die—they respawn.

- Powered by Redstone!

- A diamond in your hand is worth two in a lava pool!

- Minecraft: so many blocks, so little time!

- When one portal closes, another one opens!

- If a creeper is in range, then so are you!

- "I'm not retreating! I'm advancing in another direction!"

- Minecraft: from the ground up!

- Don't just build it, create!

- May the Minecraft be with you!

- And another mob bites the dust!

- Be in Creative mode, play in adventure!

AUTHOR BIOS

Michele C. Hollow is an award-winning writer who learned about Minecraft from her son, Jordon. She blogs at *Pet News and Views* and is the author of several children's books. She has absolutely no sense of humour, which her husband and son find ironic, but she doesn't get.

Jordon P. Hollow plays Minecraft every chance he gets. An avid reader, especially on the subject of Minecraft, Jordon loves macaroni cheese, cheese toasties, and Tastykake pies. He is a student.

Steven M. Hollow is an accomplished writer, actor, storyteller, puppeteer, and teaching artist. He began playing video games with the original introduction of Pong and plans to move on to other video games once he figures out how to move the paddles.